inside
the
mind
of
awareness

selections from
        Marcus Aurelius
        Meher Baba
        Jesus
        Buddha

compiled by
peter ingle

inside the mind of awareness

Inside the Mind of Awareness
Selections from Marcus Aurelius,
Meher Baba, Jesus, and Buddha

Copyright © 2012–2017 by Peter Ingle
All Rights Reserved

No part of this publication may be reproduced, store, or transmitted, in any form, or by any means, electronic, mechanical, photocopying, recording, or otherwise, without permission in writing from the author.

Library of Congress Cataloging-in-Publication Data

Ingle, Peter M.
Inside the Mind of Awareness
Selections from Marcus Aurelius,
Meher Baba, Jesus, and Buddha

ISBN 978-0-9746349-7-5
Produced in the United States

Awareness resides beyond the mind and encompasses the mind. Through perception, the mysterious world of awareness is reflected in the psychological world of thought, which subsequently reverberates in the physical world as speech and action.

The selections in this book are meant to demonstrate that even the most profound thoughts are not the source they spring from. They reflect that source, point to it, and urge us toward it—toward the simple, pure presence of an awareness just beyond thoughts, and just behind the eyes seeing *and* reading them.

That is what this book is about.

inside the mind of awareness

inside the mind of awareness

Selections from Marcus Aurelius 1

Selections from Meher Baba 29

Selections from Jesus 55

Selections from Buddha 77

inside the mind of awareness

Selections from
Marcus Aurelius

inside the mind of awareness

RETURN to thy sober senses and call thy self back.

A limit of time is fixed for thee, which if thou dost not use for clearing away the clouds from thy mind, it will go and thou wilt go, and it will never return.

Adapt thy self to the things with which thy lot has been cast.

Do not be whirled about. Do not disturb thy self. Make thy self all simplicity.

Thou wilt give thy self relief if thou doest every act of thy life as if it were the last.

No longer be pulled by the strings like a puppet; no longer be dissatisfied with thy present lot, or shrink from the future.

Bear in mind that every man lives only this present time, and that all the rest of his life is either past or uncertain.

The present is the only thing of which a man can be deprived.

Nothing so elevates the mind as to examine methodically every object which is presented to thee in life, so as to see what kind of universe this is and what kind of use everything performs in it.

It is peculiar to the good man to be pleased and content with what happens.

Life is a warfare and a stranger's sojourn.

Nowhere either with more quiet or more freedom from trouble does a man retire than into his own soul. Constantly give to thy self this retreat, and renew thy self.

It is in thy power whenever thou shalt choose to retire into thy self.

The universe is transformation; life is opinion.

Let thy principles be brief and fundamental, which, as soon as thou shalt recur to them, will be sufficient to cleanse the soul completely, and to send thee back free from all discontent with the things to which thou returnest.

Tranquility is nothing else than the good ordering of the mind.

Be sober in thy relaxation.

Everything which happens, happens justly, and if thou observest carefully, thou wilt find it to be so.

Within ten days thou wilt seem a god to those to whom thou art now a beast, if thou wilt return to thy principles.

Things do not touch the soul; our perturbations come only from the opinion which is within.

Thou wilt soon die, and thou art yet not simple, nor free from perturbations, nor without suspicion of being hurt by external things, nor kindly disposed towards all; nor dost thou yet place wisdom only in acting justly.

How much trouble he avoids who does not look to see what his neighbour says or does or thinks, but only to what he does himself, that it may be just and pure.

Love the art, poor as it may be, which thou hast learned, and be content with it; pass through the rest of life like one who has entrusted to the gods all that he has, making thy self neither the tyrant nor the slave of any man.

Try how the life of the good man suits thee; the life of him who is satisfied with his portion out of the whole, and with his own just acts and benevolent disposition.

Constantly regard the universe as one living being having one substance and one soul; and observe how all things have reference to one perception, the perception of this one living being.

Remember on every occasion that leads thee to vexation to apply this principle: not that this is a misfortune, but that to bear it nobly is good fortune.

That which happens to thee was done for thee and prescribed for thee, and in a manner had reference to thee, originally from the most ancient causes spun with thy destiny.

How easy it is to repel and to wipe away every impression which is troublesome or unsuitable, and immediately to be in all tranquility.

Return to philosophy frequently and repose in her.

Such as are thy habitual thoughts, such also will be the character of thy mind; for the soul is dyed by the thoughts.

We ought to lay things bare and look at their worthlessness, and strip them of all the words by which they are exalted.

Be not ashamed to be helped.

When thou hast been compelled by circumstances to be disturbed in a manner, quickly return to thy self and do not continue out of tune longer than the compulsion lasts; for thou wilt have more mastery over the harmony by continually recurring to it.

Live with the gods. And he does live with the gods who constantly shows to them that his own soul is satisfied with that which is assigned to him.

To reverence and honour thy own mind will make thee content with thy self, and in harmony with society, and in agreement with the gods.

Frequently consider the connection of all things in the universe.

Death is a cessation of the impressions through the senses.

If any man is able to convince me that I do not think or act rightly, I will gladly change; for I seek the truth, by which no man was ever injured.

The best way of avenging thy self is not to become like the wrong doer.

On all occasions call on the gods.

We are all working together to one end, some with knowledge and design, and others without knowing what they do.

Accustom thy self to attend carefully to what is said by another, and as much as it is possible, be in the speaker's mind.

Keep the ruling faculty in its own power.

Every man is worth just so much as the things are worth about which he busies himself.

Nothing will happen to thee contrary to the reason of the universe.

Things themselves have no natural power to form our judgements.

Consider thyself to be dead and to have completed thy life up to the present time, and live according to nature the remainder which is allowed thee.

The ruling faculty does not disturb itself and in itself wants nothing; therefore, it is free from perturbation and unimpeded.

Wipe out the imagination. Stop the pulling of the strings. Confine thy self to the present.

At all times it is in thy power to acquiesce in thy present condition, and to behave justly to those who are about thee, and to exert thy skill upon thy present thoughts, that nothing shall steal into them without being well examined.

Let the wrong which is done by a man stay there where the wrong was done.

Think of thy last hour. Adorn thy self with simplicity and modesty.

Love that only which happens to thee and is spun with the thread of thy destiny. For what is more suitable?

Every soul is involuntarily deprived of truth. Bear this constantly in mind, and thou wilt be more gentle towards all.

Stand ready and firm to meet onsets which are sudden and unexpected.

Be not perturbed, for all things are according to the nature of the universe. Everything exists for some end.

Look within. Within is the fountain of good, and it will ever bubble up, if thou wilt ever dig.

Speak to every man appropriately and without affectation. Use plain discourse.

If thou art pained by any external thing, it is not this thing that disturbs, but thy own judgement about it.

The ruling faculty when self-collected is satisfied with itself.

Attend to the matter which is before thee.

When men blame thee or hate thee, or say about thee anything injurious, approach their souls, penetrate within, and see what kind of men they are. Thou wilt discover that there is no reason to take any trouble that they may have this or that opinion about thee.

He who does wrong does wrong to himself. But perhaps he has not done wrong.

What harm is done if the uninstructed man does the acts of an uninstructed man? Consider whether thou shouldst not rather blame thyself because thou didst not expect such a man to err in such a way.

Man and God and the universe produce fruit at the proper seasons.

Does a man please himself who repents of nearly everything he does?

Thou hast endured infinite troubles through not being contented with thy ruling faculty.

In a word, if there is a god, all is well; and if chance rules, do not thou also be governed by it.

The mind which is free from passions is a citadel.

On the occasion of anything being done by any person, inquire with thy self: "for what object is this man doing this?" But begin with thy self; examine thy self first.

Be content if the smallest thing goes on well, and consider such an event to be no small matter.

Wilt thou never be good and simple and one and naked? Wilt thou never enjoy an affectionate and contented disposition? Wilt thou never be full and without a want of any kind?

When thou art offended at any man's fault, forthwith turn to thy self and reflect in what like manner thou dost err thyself.

That which is evil to thee and harmful has its foundation only in the mind.

Convince thy self that thou hast everything and that it comes from the gods, that everything is well for thee, and will be well whatever shall please them.

Consider that thou dost not understand whether men are doing wrong or not, for many things are done with a certain reference to circumstance.

Endure and toil without complaining.

It will greatly help thee if thou rememberest the gods, and that they wish not to be flattered, but wish all reasonable beings to be made like themselves.

The healthy understanding ought to be prepared for everything which happens.

In contemplating thy self, never include the vessel which surrounds thee.

If thou seest clear, go by this way content without turning back; but if thou dost not see clear, stop and take the best advisers. But if any other things oppose thee, go on according to thy powers with due consideration, keeping to that which appears to be just. For it is best to reach this object, and if thou dost fail, let thy failure be in attempting this.

Only to the rational animal is it given to follow voluntarily what happens; but simply to follow is a necessity imposed on all.

A man must learn a great deal to enable him to pass a correct judgement on another man's acts.

Who is he that shall hinder thee from being good and simple?

Take no notice of the past and trust the future to providence.

All is opinion and opinion is in thy power. Take away, then, thy opinion and, like a mariner who has doubled the promontory, thou wilt find calm, everything stable, and a waveless bay.

How does the ruling faculty make use of itself? For all lies in this. Everything else is lifeless ashes and smoke.

Reverence that which is highest in thy self.

No longer talk about the kind of man that a good man ought to be, but be such.

Strive to live only what is really thy life, that is, the present.

Selections from Meher Baba

DO NOT worry about anything. Be cheerful, be honest, and look after your health.

Be perfectly frank and honest. Speak from your heart.

Honesty is the keynote to divinity.

I am that which is not body, energy, or mind.

Explanations and understandings mean that you drive away god instead of drawing him in.

Hafiz said, "God is like the bird of Paradise. Don't try to snare him by spreading the net of thoughts. In that net you will find nothing but mind. Only love, and god will be yours."

Unless you learn to love in its true sense, you cannot cross the hurdle of the mind.

To love means to lose your whole self with all its paraphernalia.

Losing oneself and finding oneself is for very few lovers who carry their lives in their sleeves.

You have to become what you already are. Through love you become what you already are.

Unless you lose 'I' you cannot see and become god.

Your work has to be defined. It has to be practical and yet divine.

It is your mind that binds you. It is also the mind that is the means of your freedom. You are eternally free. You are not bound at all.

Obedience is greater than love and surrender of the mind is greater than obedience.

Love for god and obedience to a master are beyond the reach of man on his own, and complete surrender is almost impossible. The best thing is for man to purify his heart.

Only through the help and grace of a perfect master can the ego be dissolved.

God has not come out of the universe. The universe has come out of god.

The best way to cleanse the heart and to prepare for the stilling of the mind is to lead a normal life in the world.

Living in the midst of your day-to-day duties, responsibilities, likes and dislikes, becomes the very means for the perfection of your heart.

Leave your thoughts alone, but maintain constant vigil over your actions.

Let thoughts come and go without putting them into action.

Although your mind may be angry, do not let your heart know it. Remain unaffected. Then the related impressions in your mind begin to wear out and become less harmful.

Remember others with kindness and generosity, and forget yourself.

Not through desperate self-seeking, but through constant self-giving will you find the self of all selves.

Give up parrotry in all its aspects. Start practicing whatever you feel truly to be true and justly to be just.

Meditation is neither devotion nor love.

Be more aggressive towards yourself and more tolerant of others.

It is not what you believe, but what you are that will ultimately count.

Consciousness, loaded with attachments, gets pinned to the sense-world.

Only when your mind is utterly detached from the false is it possible for you to disentangle yourself from the repetitive clutches of the fleeting moment.

The real center of experience is god.

Rise above the limited self of the separative ego-mind. Realize that you are one with the limitless Truth.

In order to know the self as it is, consciousness has to be completely freed from the limitations of the individual mind.

The individual mind has to disappear, but consciousness has to be retained.

Consciousness has come to be embedded in the individual mind and cannot be extricated from this setting into which it has been woven. The result is that, if the mind is stilled, consciousness also disappears (as when you try to stop mental activity through meditation and you become unconscious—fall asleep).

The limited mind is the soil in which the ego is securely rooted.

Consciousness is mind-ridden.

A desire to know one's true nature cannot lead to the truth as long as the burden of the ego is placed upon consciousness.

The ego is the center of all human activity.

The ego is unable to end its own existence. All that it does to bring about self-annihilation only goes to add to its own existence. It flourishes on the very efforts directed against itself.

The unrealized soul is still subject to the illusion of the universe.

When the individual mind is dissolved, the whole universe relative to the mind vanishes into nothingness, and consciousness is no longer tied to anything.

The problem of god-realization is the problem of emancipating consciousness from the limitations of the mind.

God-realization is a personal state of consciousness belonging to, and having significance only for, the soul that has transcended the domain of the mind.

The ego attempts the integration of experience, but it does so around the false idea of separateness.

Life cannot be understood and lived fully as long as it is made to move around the pivot of the ego.

After the attainment of god-realization, the soul discovers that it has always been the infinite reality that it now knows itself to be, and that its regarding itself as finite during the period of evolution was in fact an illusion. All that it has been through was but the process of finding itself.

Spiritual freedom consists in internal renunciation and not in external renunciation, but external renunciation is a great aid in achieving internal renunciation.

The ego is an affirmation of separateness. It affirms its separateness through craving, hate, anger, fears, or jealousy. Every thought, feeling, or action that springs from the idea of separate or exclusive existence nourishes the sense of 'I.'

Love alone is inclusive, which helps bridge the artificial gulf of separateness.

The ego is made of variegated desires, and the destroying of these desires amounts to the destruction of the ego.

The ego is like an iceberg; only about one-seventh is visible. The major portion remains submerged in the dark and inarticulate sanctuaries of the subconscious mind.

The roots of the ego are in the subconscious mind in the form of latent tendencies.

Digging out the buried roots of the ego from the deeper layers of the subconscious mind and bringing them to the light of consciousness is one important part of the process of wiping out the ego. But dealing with them is by no means clear and simple because the ego has a tendency to live through any of the opposites of experience. It thereby eludes the attack of intelligent consciousness and perpetuates itself.

Aggressiveness is a natural outcome of the need to compensate for the poverty of the ego life.

In the more advanced stages of the path, the ego does not seek to maintain itself through open methods (pride, vanity, slander), but takes shelter in those very things that are pursued for the slimming down of the ego (humility, spirituality, denial). These tactics are like guerilla warfare.

The ousting of the ego from consciousness is necessarily an intricate process and cannot be achieved by exercising a constantly uniform approach. The ego has almost infinite possibilities for making its existence secure and for creating self-delusion.

The ego as an affirmation of separateness lives through the idea of "mine."

The ego seeks self-expression in inferiority and superiority, which are reactions to each other; or in equality, which is a reaction to both. Beyond all of these is the reality of unity.

The ego gauges superiority and inferiority in terms of possessions, achievements, rank.

Appreciation of the divinity of the master is the manner in which the higher self of the disciple expresses its sense of dignity.

Consciousness must draw its directive momentum not from the ego, but from some other principle.

It is futile to try to glean knowledge of true values by exercise of the mind alone.

All concepts that the intellect evolves for knowledge of material things are inadequate for understanding the spirit.

Matter is understood through the mind working upon data given through the different senses, but spirit can be understood only through the spirit.

The best approach for the understanding of the spirit is through the heart.

The heart has glimpses of the unity of the spirit.

If you want to be certain about the object of love before giving your love, it is only a form of calculating selfishness.

When the mind seeks conviction or corroboration, it is encroaching upon the sphere that properly belongs to the heart.

You cannot love through the intellect.

When a person has his eye on the results of actions instead of being concerned solely with their intrinsic worth, he is trying to tackle spiritual problems through the mind alone, and in doing so is interfering with the proper functioning of the heart.

Spirituality does not consist in intellectual knowledge of true values, but in their realization.

The intellect of most persons is harnessed by innumerable wants, yet lasting happiness dawns only where there is complete freedom from wants.

Wants mean denial of the life of the spirit.

The mind is the treasure house of learning, but the heart is the treasure house of spiritual wisdom.

You have to go beyond the mind to experience the spiritual bliss of desirelessness.

Only when the mind accepts its ends and values from the deepest promptings of the heart does it contribute to the life of the spirit. Factual knowledge has to be subordinated to intuitive perceptions, and the heart has to be allowed full freedom in determining the ends of life without any interference from the mind.

The mind has a place in practical life, but its role begins after the heart has had its say.

Shall we go on explaining, or shall we be quiet?

Selections from Jesus

CONSIDER how long the world
Has existed before you,
And how long it will last after you.
Then you will discover that
Your life lasts but a day,
And your suffering but a single hour.

Will you not forsake the love of flesh and
The fear of suffering?
Do you not know?
You have not yet been insulted,
You have not yet been accused falsely,
You have not yet been thrown into prison,
You have not yet been condemned unjustly,
You have not yet been crucified
Without reason,
And you have not yet been buried
In the ground,
As I was.

Remember my cross and my death,
And you will live.

Seek after death as the dead seek after life.

What is truly good will never be a part
Of this world.

Do your best to be saved without any urging.
Rather, spur yourselves on, and reach the goal
Before me if you can.

There is nothing hidden
That will not be revealed.

Do not let the kingdom of heaven waste away.
Do not let the kingdom of heaven become
A desert in you.

No one will persecute you
And no one will oppress you,
Unless you do this to yourselves.

Do not lie or do what you dislike.

You are loved ones.
You will bring life to many people.

Blessed are those who have grown confident
And have found grace for themselves.

Remember that I was with you
And you did not know me.

Blessed are those who have known me.
Blessed are those who have not seen
But yet have believed.

Again I admonish you, you who exist:
Be like those who do not exist,
That you may dwell with those
Who do not exist.

Do not be proud because of the light
That brings enlightenment.

I tell you the truth:
Whoever receives life
And believes in the kingdom
Will never leave the kingdom,
Not even if the Father wishes to
Cast such a person out.

Know what is within your sight,
And what is hidden from you
Will become clear to you.

Do you think that many have found
The kingdom of heaven?

When you become enlightened,
What will you do?

Whoever is close to me is close to the fire.

The wise fisher discovered a fine big fish.
So he threw all the little fish back into the sea,
And with no hesitation kept the big fish.
Whoever has ears to hear ought to listen.

I shall give you what no eye has seen,
What no ear has heard,
What no hand has touched,
And what has never arisen in a human mind.

Be on guard against the world.
Gird yourselves and prepare for action.

Love your companion like your life.

When you take the beam out of your own eye,
Then you will see well enough to take
The speck out of your companion's eye.

Do not worry from morning to evening,
And from evening to morning,
About what you will wear.

Often you have desired to have these sayings
That I am telling you.
There will be days you will seek me
But will not find me.

Blessed is one who has suffered.
That one has found life.

I disclose my mysteries to those
Who are worthy of my mysteries.

Whoever has come to know the world
Has discovered a carcass,
And whoever has discovered a carcass
Is worth more than the world.

Whoever knows everything,
But lacks within,
Lacks everything.

Be attentive!

If you bring forth what is within you,
What you have will save you.

There was a rich farmer
Who had a great deal of money.
The farmer said,
'I shall invest my money so
That I may sow, reap, plant, and
Fill my storehouses.
Then I shall have everything.'
Those were the plans,
But that very night the farmer died.
Whoever has ears ought to listen.

Seek a place of rest in yourselves,
That you may not become a carcass
And be eaten.

Seek after the treasure that is unfailing,
That is abiding,
Where no moth comes to consume,
And no worm destroys.

The harvest is large
But the workers are few.

Examine yourself and understand
Who you are,
How you live,
And what will become of you.

No one among you will ever enter
The kingdom because I commanded it,
But rather because you yourselves are filled.

Be filled and let there be
No empty space within you.

One person who is lacking
Is not filled in the same way as another.

Be filled with spirit
But lacking in human reason,
For human reason is only human reason.

Whoever does not know self
Does not know anything.
But whoever knows self
Already has acquired knowledge
About the depths of the universe.

Whatever is subject to change
Will perish and be lost.

Blessed is the wise person who seeks truth.
When one finds it,
One rests upon it forever,
And is not afraid of those
Who want to disturb one.

Some people run after what they can see,
What is far from truth.
The fire that leads them will give
An illusion of truth,
And will shine on them with
Transitory beauty.
It will make them prisoners of
The delights of darkness.
It will make them blind with
Unquenchable passion.
It will inflame their souls.

What is visible in human existence
Will pass away.
The fleshy body of people
Will pass away.
And when it disintegrates,
It will find its place in what is visible
And can be seen.

There is but a little time before
What you can see will pass away.

People, being foolish and mad,
Are happy in the anxieties of this life.
Some of those who rush into this madness
Do not realize they are foolish,
But think they are wise.
They are drawn to the beauty of the body,
As if it would not perish.
Their minds turn to themselves,
Their thoughts are on their pursuits,
But the fire will consume them.

You do not realize how
The moon looks down
Night and day
And sees your slaughtered bodies.

Blessed are you who know beforehand
About what may entrap you,
And who flee what is alien to you.

Watch and pray
That you may not be born in the flesh,
But that you may leave the bitter bondage
Of this life.

The kingdom of heaven is within you.

If you do not fast from the world,
You will not find the kingdom.

Learn how to suffer
And you shall be able not to suffer.

The One is a sovereign
That has nothing over it.
It is the God and Father of all.
It is illimitable, since there is nothing
Before it to limit it.
It is unutterable, since nothing could
Comprehend it to utter it.
It is eternal, and exists eternally.
It is immeasurable light,
Pure, holy, bright.
What shall I tell you about it?
It is quiet,
It is at rest,
And it is before everything.
It is the head of all the worlds and
It sustains them through its goodness.

Do not be fainthearted.

Endure everything and bear everything
So as to finish the contest and
Obtain eternal life.

When you leave bodily pains and passions,
You will receive rest from the Good One,
And you will reign with the King,
You united with the King,
And the King united with you,
Now and for ever
And ever.

Selections from Buddha

SPEAK or act with a pure mind
And happiness will follow you
As your shadow, unshakable.

You too shall pass away.
Knowing this, how can you quarrel?

Only love dispels hate.

Look into your heart.
Follow your nature.

Know the truth and find peace.

Awake, reflect, and watch.
Work with care and attention.

Never offend
By what you say, or do, or think.

The master guards his watching.
It is his most precious treasure.

How wonderful it is to watch.
How foolish to sleep.

The master makes for himself an island
Which the flood cannot overwhelm.
The fool who knows he is a fool
Is that much wiser.

An untroubled mind,
No longer seeking to consider
What is right and what is wrong,
Watches and understands.

Know that the body is a fragile jar,
And make a castle of your mind.
On every trial
Let understanding fight for you
To defend what you have won.

How hard it is to serve your self.

Your worst enemy cannot harm you
As much as your own thoughts, unguarded.
But once mastered,
No one can help you as much.

Soon the body is discarded.
Then what does it feel?
A useless log of wood, it lies on the ground.
Then what does it know?

Nowhere can you hide from your own death.

Snap the flower arrows of desire
And then, unseen,
Escape the king of death.
And travel on.

Look to your own faults.
Overlook the faults of others.

With single-mindedness
The master quells his thoughts.
He ends their wandering.
Seated in the cave of the heart,
He finds freedom.

Look not for recognition
But follow the awakened
And set yourself free.

The farmer channels water to his land.
The fletcher whittles his arrows.
And the carpenter turns his wood.
So the wise man directs his mind.

Want nothing.
Where there is desire,
Say nothing.

Happiness or sorrow—
Whatever befalls you,
Walk on
Untouched, unattached.

Few cross over the river.
Most are stranded on this side.
On the riverbank they run up and down.
But the wise man, following the way,
Crosses over, beyond the reach of death.

Those who awaken
Never rest in one place.
Like swans, they rise
And leave the lake.

The master surrenders his beliefs.
He sees beyond the end and the beginning.
He cuts all ties.
He gives up all desires.
He resists all temptations.
And he rises.

Even in the empty forest
He finds joy
Because he wants nothing.

It is better to conquer yourself
Than to win a thousand battles.
Then the victory is yours.

Better than a hundred years of idleness
Is one day spent in determination.
Better to live one day
Wondering how all things arise and pass away.

A jug fills drop by drop.
So the wise man becomes brimful of virtue.

Like a noble horse
Smart under the whip,
Burn and be swift.

See yourself in others.
Then whom can you hurt?
What harm can you do?

Like a broken gong
Be still, be silent.
Know the stillness of freedom
Where there is no more striving.

The pure are not reborn.

The ignorant man is an ox.
He grows in size, not wisdom.

The world is on fire!
And are you laughing?

Behold your body—
A painted puppet, a toy,
Jointed and sick and full of false imaginings,
A shadow that shifts and fades.
Like every living thing
In the end it sickens and dies.
And are you laughing?

The wise man masters himself.

Love yourself, and watch—
Today, tomorrow, always.

You are your only master.
Who else?
Subdue yourself,
And discover your master.

Never offend
By what you say, or do, or think.

You are the source
Of all purity and all impurity.

No one purifies another.

Speak the truth.
Give whatever you can.
Never be angry.
These three steps will lead you
Into the presence of the gods.

Your life is falling away.
Death is at hand.
You are to travel far away.
What will you take with you?

Unrepaired the house falls into ruin,
And the watch, without vigilance, fails.

The way is not in the sky.
The way is in the heart.

See how you love
Whatever keeps you from your journey.

All things arise and pass away.
But the awakened awake forever.

It is not good conduct
That helps you upon the way,
Nor ritual, nor book learning,
Nor withdrawal into the self,
Nor deep meditation.
None of these confers mastery or joy.

O seeker!
Rely on nothing
Until you want nothing.

Outwit desire.

All virtue lies in detachment.

It is you who must make the effort.
The masters only point the way.

Never neglect your work
For another's,
However great his need.

Your work is to discover your work
And then with all your heart
To give yourself to it.

A man may grow old in vain.

Arise and watch.

Consider the world —
A bubble, a mirage.
See the world as it is,
And death shall overlook you.

As the moon slips from behind the cloud
And shines,
So the master comes out
From behind his ignorance
And shines.

At the end of the Way is freedom.
Till then, patience.

The awakened are few and hard to find.

Look within.
Be still.

Like nothing lest you lose it.
Free yourself from attachment.

Let go of anger.
Let go of pride.
When you are bound by nothing
You go beyond sorrow.

With gentleness overcome anger.
With generosity overcome meanness.
With truth overcome deceit.

Understand, and go beyond sorrow.
Existence is illusion.

Arise!
Lest through irresolution and idleness
You lose the Way.

Fell desire
And set yourself free.
If your purpose wavers,
You will not find light.

Sit.
Rest.
Work.
Alone with yourself,
Never weary.

It is hard to live in the world
And hard to live out of it.

Give yourself to the journey.

Like a border town well guarded,
Guard yourself within and without.

Awake.
Be the witness of your thoughts.

Do not carry with you your mistakes.
Do not carry your cares.

It is sweet to live arduously
And to master yourself.

If you subdue desire
Your sorrows fall from you.

Abandon yesterday, and tomorrow,
And today.
Cross over to the farther shore,
Beyond life and death.

Quieten your mind.
Reflect.
Watch.
Nothing binds you.
You are free.

The end of desire is the end of sorrow.

Seek rather the other shore.

In all things be a master
Of what you do and say and think.
Be free.

Give thanks
For what has been given you,
However little.

Do not reach out for what is given to others,
Lest you disturb your quietness.

You have no name and no form.
Why miss what you do not have?

Seeker!
Empty the boat,
Lighten the load,
And sail swiftly.

Do not be reckless.
Meditate constantly.

With a quiet mind,
Come into that empty house,
Your heart.

Let fall willfulness and hatred.

By your own efforts
Waken yourself, watch yourself.

Like the moon,
Come out from behind the clouds.
Shine!

Be quiet.
Do your work, with mastery.

Honor the man who is awake
And shows you the way.
Honor the fire of his sacrifice.

Cut through
The strap and throng and the rope.
Loosen the fastenings.
Unbolt the doors of sleep,
And awake.

A master does not cling.

A master wants nothing from this world
And nothing from the next.
He is free.

Other books by Peter Ingle

OUR FATHER
Talks About the Inner Meaning of
The Lord's Prayer with Temerlen P. Gillis

The Heart of Awareness

The Little Book of Awareness

The Little Book of
Transforming Negative Emotions

Think Before You Write

www.ingramcontent.com/pod-product-compliance
Lightning Source LLC
Chambersburg PA
CBHW020658300426
44112CB00007B/439